Gardening

the Art

A book by

Allen Nissanth

CONTENTS

CHAPTER 1
INTRODUCTION

Gardening is the art and practice of cultivating and nurturing plants, whether for practical, aesthetic, or recreational purposes. It involves a wide range of activities, from planting and growing vegetables, fruits, herbs, and flowers to maintaining lawns and landscaping. Gardening can take place in various settings, such as private gardens, community plots, urban spaces, and even indoor environments.

Gardening offers numerous benefits beyond the beauty it brings to outdoor spaces. It provides a way to connect with nature, promote sustainability, and improve mental and physical well-being. Whether you're a seasoned gardener with a green thumb or a beginner looking to dip your toes into this rewarding hobby, there's always something new to learn and explore in the world of gardening.

Throughout history, gardening has played a significant role in various cultures, serving as a source of sustenance, medicine, and artistic expression. From ancient civilizations to modern times, people have practiced gardening to provide food, create beautiful landscapes, and enhance their living environments.

Gardening encompasses a wide range of activities, including soil preparation, planting, watering, fertilizing, pruning, pest control, and harvesting. Different types of gardens cater to specific interests and needs, such as vegetable gardens for homegrown produce, flower gardens for ornamental beauty, and herb gardens for culinary and medicinal herbs.

As you delve into the world of gardening, you'll discover the joy of watching plants flourish under your care, the satisfaction of reaping the rewards of your efforts, and the sense of connection to the natural world. Whether you're tending to a small balcony garden, a sprawling backyard oasis, or a community plot, gardening is a fulfilling and enriching endeavor that allows you to create and nurture life while enjoying the beauty and tranquility of the outdoors.

CHAPTER 2

PLANNING YOUR GARDEN

Planning your garden is a crucial first step in creating a successful and enjoyable gardening experience. A well-thought-out plan can help you make the most of your space, time, and resources, and ultimately lead to a beautiful and productive garden. Here's a step-by-step guide to help you in planning your garden:

CHOOSE YOUR GARDEN TYPE:

Decide what type of garden you want to create. Are you interested in a vegetable garden, flower garden, herb garden, or a combination of these? Each type of garden has its own requirements and considerations.

SELECT A LOCATION:

Assess your available space for gardening. Consider factors such as sunlight exposure, soil quality, drainage, and proximity to water sources. Different plants have different sunlight requirements, so choose a location that suits the plants you want to grow.

SET GOALS:

Determine your gardening goals. Are you aiming to grow your own food, create a serene outdoor retreat, attract pollinators, or simply enjoy the beauty of plants? Your goals will influence the layout and design of your garden.

DRAW A GARDEN LAYOUT:

Sketch a rough layout of your garden space. Consider the arrangement of beds, pathways, and any structures you might want to include, like trellises or raised beds. This will give you a visual representation of your garden's design.

CHOOSE PLANTS:

Research and choose plants that are well-suited to your climate, soil type, and available sunlight. Consider factors like plant size, growth habits, and maintenance requirements. Group plants with similar needs together to make watering and care more efficient.

CONSIDER SEASONALITY:

Plan for year-round interest by selecting plants that offer visual appeal in different seasons. This could include spring-flowering bulbs, summer annuals, fall foliage, and winter evergreens.

SOIL PREPARATION:

Test your soil's pH and nutrient levels. Amend the soil as needed to create a fertile and well-draining growing environment for your plants.

CREATE A PLANTING SCHEDULE:

Determine the best times for planting based on your local climate and growing season. Some plants are best started from seeds indoors before transplanting, while others can be directly sown into the garden.

IMPLEMENT WATERING & IRRIGATION:

Decide on a watering schedule and method. Consider using drip irrigation, soaker hoses, or other water-efficient systems to ensure plants receive adequate moisture.

PLAN FOR MAINTENANCE:

Factor in ongoing maintenance tasks, such as weeding, pruning, fertilizing, and pest control. Regular care is essential for the health and vitality of your garden.

INCLUDE HARDSCAPING ELEMENTS:

Integrate pathways, seating areas, and other hardscaping features into your garden design to enhance its functionality and aesthetics.

BUDGET AND RESOURCES:

Estimate the costs associated with your garden plan, including plants, tools, materials, and any additional features. Allocate your resources wisely to ensure a successful garden without overspending.

START SMALL:

If you're new to gardening, consider starting with a small area or a few containers. This will help you gain experience and build your skills gradually.

CHAPTER 3

SEEDINGS AND SEEDLINGS

Seeds and seedlings are fundamental components of gardening, serving as the starting point for growing plants in your garden. Understanding how to properly handle, sow, and care for seeds and seedlings is essential for a successful gardening experience. Here's a guide to help you work with seeds and seedlings effectively:

SEEDS:

SELECTING SEEDS:

Choose high-quality seeds from reputable sources. Consider factors such as plant variety, growth habits, disease resistance, and suitability for your climate.

STARTING SEEDS INDOORS:

Some plants benefit from being started indoors before being transplanted into the garden. Use seed trays or pots filled with a seed-starting mix. Follow the seed packet's instructions for planting depth and spacing.

SOWING SEEDS OUTDOORS:

For plants that are directly sown into the garden, prepare the soil by loosening it and removing any debris. Follow the recommended planting depth and spacing on the seed packet.

GERMINATION:

Seeds need the right conditions to germinate. Ensure they receive adequate moisture, warmth, and light. A seedling heat mat and grow lights can help provide consistent conditions for germination.

THINNING:

Once seedlings have sprouted, thin them out to provide enough space for proper growth. Remove weaker seedlings to avoid overcrowding.

HARDENING OFF:

Before transplanting seedlings outdoors, gradually acclimate them to outdoor conditions. Place them outside for increasingly longer periods each day, starting in a sheltered spot.

SEEDLINGS:

TRANSPLANTING:

When seedlings are strong and have developed a few sets of true leaves, they're ready to be transplanted into the garden. Choose a cloudy day or transplant in the evening to reduce transplant shock.

PREPARING THE SOIL:

Dig a hole in the garden soil slightly larger than the seedling's root ball. Gently remove the seedling from its container, being careful not to disturb the roots. Place the seedling in the hole and fill with soil, pressing lightly to secure it.

WATERING:

Water the newly transplanted seedlings immediately after planting. Provide consistent moisture as they establish themselves in their new environment.

MULCHING:

Apply a layer of organic mulch around the base of seedlings to help retain soil moisture, suppress weeds, and regulate soil temperature.

SUPPORT AND PRUNING:

Some seedlings, like tomatoes or peppers, may require staking or support as they grow. Pinch back the tips of certain seedlings to encourage bushier growth.

FERTILIZING:

Depending on the type of plants, you may need to provide additional nutrients as seedlings grow. Follow recommended fertilization guidelines for your specific plants.

PROTECTION:

Be vigilant about protecting young seedlings from pests and adverse weather conditions. Use physical barriers, row covers, or organic pest control methods as needed.

By giving proper attention to your seeds and seedlings, you're laying the foundation for a thriving garden. As they grow into mature plants, you'll enjoy the satisfaction of watching your garden flourish and produce bountiful harvests or beautiful blooms. Remember that each plant type has unique requirements, so always refer to specific guidelines provided on seed packets or reliable gardening resources.

CHAPTER 4

NURTURING YOUR GARDEN

Nurturing your garden involves ongoing care, maintenance, and attention to ensure the health, growth, and vitality of your plants. Regular nurturing practices contribute to a flourishing garden that's both visually appealing and productive. Here are essential steps to effectively nurture your garden:

WATERING:

Provide consistent and appropriate watering for your plants. Different plants have different water requirements, so be sure to water according to their needs. Water deeply and at the base of the plants to encourage strong root development.

MULCHING:

Apply organic mulch, such as straw or wood chips, around your plants. Mulch helps retain soil moisture, regulate temperature, suppress weeds, and improve soil structure.

WEEDING:

Regularly remove weeds from your garden beds. Weeds compete with your plants for water, nutrients, and sunlight. Regular weeding prevents them from taking over and harming your plants.

FERTILIZING:

Feed your plants with appropriate fertilizers to provide essential nutrients. Follow recommended fertilization schedules based on plant types and growth stages. Consider using organic fertilizers to promote soil health.

PRUNING AND DEADHEADING:

Prune plants to remove dead or diseased branches and promote healthy growth. Deadhead spent flowers to encourage continuous blooming and direct energy toward new growth.

SUPPORT AND TRAINING:

Some plants, like tomatoes or climbing vines, may require staking, trellising, or other supports. Proper support helps prevent plants from bending or breaking under their own weight.

PEST AND DISEASE MANAGEMENT:

Regularly inspect your plants for signs of pests or diseases. Address issues promptly using integrated pest management techniques, which may include physical barriers, beneficial insects, or organic sprays.

HARVESTING:

Harvest ripe fruits, vegetables, and herbs in a timely manner. Regular harvesting encourages more production and prevents over-ripening, which can attract pests.

ROTATE CROPS:

If you have a vegetable garden, practice crop rotation to prevent soil-borne diseases and maintain soil fertility. Avoid planting the same family of crops in the same spot each year.

COMPOSTING:

Start a compost pile or bin to recycle organic kitchen and garden waste into nutrient-rich compost. Incorporate compost into your garden soil to improve its structure and fertility.

MONITORING AND ADJUSTING:

Regularly observe your garden's progress and adjust your care routine as needed. Be attentive to changes in plant health, growth, and environmental conditions.

ATTRACT BENEFICIAL WILDLIFE:

Encourage pollinators and other beneficial insects to visit your garden by planting native flowers and providing suitable habitats.

RECORD KEEPING:

Keep a gardening journal or use a digital tool to track planting dates, successes, challenges, and observations. This information can help you make informed decisions in future seasons.

CONTINUOUS LEARNING:

Stay curious and seek knowledge about gardening techniques, plant varieties, and sustainable practices. Gardening is an ongoing learning process, and there's always something new to discover.

Remember that gardening is a labor of love, and the effort you invest in nurturing your garden will be rewarded with a vibrant and thriving outdoor space. Over time, you'll develop a deeper connection to your garden and gain a greater understanding of the natural world around you.

CHAPTER 5

THE ART OF PRUNING AND TRIMMING

The art of pruning and trimming is a fundamental skill in gardening and landscaping that involves selectively cutting and shaping plants to improve their health, appearance, and overall structure. Proper pruning and trimming not only enhance the aesthetic appeal of your garden but also contribute to the well-being and longevity of your plants. Here's a guide to help you master the art of pruning and trimming:

UNDERSTAND THE PURPOSE:

Pruning: Pruning serves various purposes, including removing dead or diseased branches, encouraging new growth, shaping plants, improving airflow, and controlling size.

Trimming: Trimming generally refers to maintaining the shape and size of plants, particularly hedges, topiaries, and ornamental shrubs.

CHOOSE THE RIGHT TOOLS:

Invest in high-quality pruning tools such as bypass pruners, loppers, pruning saws, and hedge shears. Clean and sharpen your tools regularly for precise cuts and to prevent the spread of diseases.

TIMING MATTERS:

Different plants have specific times of the year when pruning is most effective. Research and understand the ideal timing for each plant species in your garden.

TECHNIQUES FOR PRUNING:

Remove Dead or Diseased Branches: Start by cutting away any dead, diseased, or damaged branches to prevent the spread of diseases and improve plant health.

Thinning: Thin out overcrowded branches to improve airflow and light penetration, reducing the risk of fungal issues.

Shaping: Use selective cuts to shape plants according to your desired aesthetic. Consider the plant's natural growth habit and prune accordingly.

Heading Back: Cut back long or unruly branches to encourage branching and denser growth.

TECHNIQUES FOR TRIMMING:

Hedge Trimming: Maintain a straight edge and level top when trimming hedges. Use a guide string for accuracy, and avoid cutting too much at once to prevent stress to the plant.

Topiary Trimming: Shape topiaries with precision, following the desired design. Regular trimming helps maintain the intricate form of the topiary.

PRUNING TIPS:

Use clean, sharp cuts: Clean cuts heal faster and reduce the risk of disease.

Prune just above a node or bud: Cutting above a node encourages new growth in the desired direction.

Angle cuts: Angle cuts slightly away from the bud to prevent water from collecting and causing rot.

Don't over-prune: Avoid removing more than a third of a plant's growth at one time to prevent stress and shock.

SAFETY PRECAUTIONS:

Wear appropriate protective gear, such as gloves and safety glasses, to prevent injuries from sharp tools or falling debris.

Use a sturdy ladder when pruning tall plants, and ensure proper footing to avoid accidents.

STEP BACK AND ASSESS:

Periodically step back and evaluate your work as you prune and trim. This helps ensure you're achieving your desired shape and overall garden aesthetic.

LEARN BY DOING:

Practice and experience are key to mastering the art of pruning and trimming. Start with simple plants and gradually work your way up to more complex ones.

Remember that pruning and trimming are skills that develop over time. Don't be afraid to make mistakes; learning from them will contribute to your growth as a gardener. As you become more confident in your abilities, you'll be able to transform your garden into a beautifully sculpted and well-maintained oasis.

CHAPTER 6

HARVESTING AND BEYOND

Harvesting is a rewarding culmination of your gardening efforts, but the process doesn't end there. What you do after harvesting plays a significant role in maximizing the benefits of your garden. From preserving your harvest to preparing for the next growing season, here's a guide to what comes after harvesting:

HARVESTING:

- Harvest crops at their peak of ripeness for the best flavor, texture, and nutritional value.
- Use clean, sharp tools to avoid damaging plants and fruits.
- Harvest herbs before they flower for the most intense flavor.
- Cut leafy greens from the outer leaves to encourage continued growth.
- Gently handle fruits and vegetables to prevent bruising.

PRESERVING YOUR HARVEST:

- Store or preserve excess produce through canning, freezing, drying, fermenting, or pickling.
- Properly label and date preserved items for easy identification.
- Share your surplus with friends, family, or local food banks.

SEED SAVING:

- Save seeds from non-hybrid plants for future plantings. Properly drying and storing seeds ensures their viability.
- Research specific seed-saving techniques for different plant varieties.

SOIL CARE AND IMPROVEMENT:

- After harvesting, amend the soil with compost or organic matter to replenish nutrients for the next growing season.

- Cover bare soil with mulch to protect it from erosion, weed growth, and temperature fluctuations.

FALL CLEANUP:

- Remove spent plants and debris from the garden to prevent pests and diseases from overwintering.
- Cut back perennials and ornamental grasses to prepare for new growth in the spring.

COVER CROPS:

Plant cover crops like clover or rye in the fall to improve soil fertility and structure during the winter months.

GARDEN MAINTENANCE:

Regularly inspect and maintain garden structures, such as trellises, stakes, and fences, to ensure their integrity.

PLANNING FOR NEXT SEASON:

- Reflect on the current season's successes and challenges to inform your plans for the next year.
- Start seedlings indoors for early spring planting.
- Prepare a garden layout and planting schedule for the upcoming season.

COMPOSTING:

Compost plant debris and kitchen scraps to create nutrient-rich compost for your garden.

CONTINUING CARE:

- Monitor plants for signs of disease or pests and take action promptly.
- Keep up with regular watering, weeding, and fertilizing as needed.

GARDEN EDUCATION:

Keep learning about gardening techniques, plant varieties, and sustainable practices to improve your skills.

ENJOY THE FRUITS OF YOUR LABOR:

Finally, savor the fresh produce you've grown, share it with loved ones, and take pride in your gardening accomplishments.

Remember that gardening is a cyclical process, and each season builds upon the lessons and experiences of the previous one. By following these post-harvest steps and continuing to care for your garden, you'll ensure a bountiful and beautiful garden year after year.

CHAPTER 7

GARDENING IN SMALL SPACES

Gardening in small spaces presents a unique set of challenges and opportunities. Whether you have a tiny balcony, a compact patio, or a small urban backyard, you can still create a thriving and beautiful garden. Here are some tips and ideas for successful gardening in limited spaces:

CHOOSE THE RIGHT PLANTS:

- Opt for compact or dwarf varieties of plants that are well-suited for small spaces.

- Consider vertical growers, such as vining plants or those that can be trellised, to maximize vertical space.

- Select plants that offer multiple benefits, such as ornamental flowers that also attract pollinators.

CONTAINER GARDENING:

- Use containers, pots, and hanging baskets to grow plants vertically and horizontally.
- Ensure containers have proper drainage and are the right size for the chosen plants.

VERTICAL GARDENING:

- Install vertical garden systems, such as wall-mounted planters or pocket planters, to utilize vertical space effectively.
- Train plants to climb trellises, arbors, or other support structures.

RAISED BEDS:

- Build raised beds to create defined growing areas and improve soil drainage.
- Stack multiple levels of raised beds for additional planting space.

COMPANION PLANTING:

Use companion planting techniques to maximize the use of available space and enhance plant health.

Plant compatible crops together to deter pests and improve pollination.

INTENSIVE PLANTING:

- Practice intensive planting by spacing plants closer together, taking advantage of every available inch of space.
- This approach minimizes bare soil, reduces weed growth, and maximizes yield.

WINDOW BOXES:

- Install window boxes on windowsills or railings to add color and greenery to your living space.
- Plant a variety of flowers, herbs, or even small vegetables.

HANGING GARDENS:

- Create hanging gardens by suspending planters from hooks, beams, or overhead structures.

- Hang cascading plants like trailing flowers or herbs for an attractive display.

UTILIZE VERTICAL SURFACES:

- Attach planters to walls, fences, or balcony railings to create a living wall or vertical garden.
- Use wall-mounted shelves or pegboards to hold potted plants or gardening tools.

COMPACT FRUIT TREES:

- Choose dwarf or mini fruit tree varieties that can be grown in containers or small spaces.
- Prune fruit trees to keep them compact and manageable.

INDOOR GARDENING:

- Bring gardening indoors with potted plants, succulents, and herbs on windowsills or shelves.
- Consider using grow lights to provide adequate light for indoor plants.

CREATIVE PLANTING:

- Get creative with your plant choices and arrangements. Combine colors, textures, and heights for an eye-catching display.

- Incorporate vertical elements like trellises, obelisks, or arches for added interest.

REGULAR MAINTENANCE:

- Regularly prune, deadhead, and thin plants to ensure they don't overcrowd each other.

- Provide consistent watering and fertilization based on the specific needs of your plants.

- Remember that gardening in small spaces requires thoughtful planning and efficient use of resources. With some creativity and careful consideration, you can transform even the tiniest of spaces into a charming and productive garden oasis.

CHAPTER 8

SUSTAINABLE AND ECO-FRIENDLY GARDENING

Sustainable and eco-friendly gardening practices are essential for reducing environmental impact, conserving resources, and creating a healthier ecosystem. By adopting these principles, you can enjoy a thriving garden while minimizing your carbon footprint and promoting biodiversity. Here are some sustainable gardening tips:

SOIL HEALTH:

- Use compost and organic matter to improve soil structure, fertility, and water retention.
- Avoid synthetic fertilizers and chemical pesticides that can harm beneficial organisms.

WATER CONSERVATION:

- Install a drip irrigation system to deliver water directly to plant roots, reducing waste.
- Collect rainwater in barrels for irrigation during dry periods.
- Mulch garden beds to retain soil moisture and suppress weed growth.

NATIVE PLANTS:

- Choose native plants adapted to your region's climate and soil conditions. They require less water and maintenance.
- Native plants also provide habitat for local wildlife and support pollinators.

BIODIVERSITY:

- Create diverse planting arrangements to attract a variety of beneficial insects, birds, and other wildlife.
- Avoid monoculture planting, which can lead to pest and disease problems.

INTEGRATED PEST MANAGEMENT (IPM):

- Use IPM techniques, such as releasing beneficial insects, introducing natural predators, and using traps, to control pests.
- Minimize pesticide use to avoid harming non-target organisms.

COMPOSTING:

- Compost kitchen scraps, yard waste, and plant debris to create nutrient-rich soil amendments.
- Reduce landfill waste and enrich your garden's soil naturally.

CHEMICAL-FREE WEED CONTROL:

- Hand-pull weeds or use mulch to suppress weed growth without relying on herbicides.

- Solarization (using sunlight to heat and kill weeds) is an eco-friendly method for weed control.

ENERGY EFFICIENCY:

- Choose manual or hand-powered tools over gas-powered ones whenever possible.
- Use solar-powered garden lights for illumination in the evening.

WILDLIFE HABITAT:

- Incorporate birdhouses, bat boxes, and bee hotels to provide shelter for beneficial creatures.
- Create water features like bird baths or small ponds to attract wildlife.

UPCYCLING AND RECYCLING:

- Repurpose items like containers, pallets, and old furniture for planters and garden structures.
- Recycle materials for garden pathways, edging, and decorative elements.

SUSTAINABLE GARDEN DESIGN:

- Plan your garden layout to make the most of natural sunlight and shade patterns.

- Position plants to create windbreaks and microclimates that optimize growing conditions.

GARDEN EDUCATION:

- Stay informed about sustainable gardening practices through workshops, books, and online resources.

- Share your knowledge with friends, family, and your community to promote eco-friendly gardening.

By implementing these sustainable gardening practices, you'll not only create a vibrant and productive garden but also contribute positively to the environment and ecosystem around you. Your garden can become a model of eco-conscious living and inspire others to adopt similar practices.

CHAPTER 9
TROUBLESHOOTING GARDEN PROBLEMS

Troubleshooting common garden problems is an important skill that every gardener should have. From pests and diseases to environmental issues, being able to identify and address problems promptly can help ensure the health and vitality of your plants. Here's a guide to help you troubleshoot and solve common garden issues:

PEST PROBLEMS:

Identification: Observe plants for signs of pests such as chewed leaves, holes, or discoloration.

Solution: Introduce beneficial insects (like ladybugs), use insecticidal soap or neem oil, or manually remove pests.

Prevention: Practice companion planting, use row covers, and maintain good garden hygiene.

DISEASE ISSUES:

Identification: Look for wilting, mold, yellowing, or spots on leaves.

Solution: Remove and dispose of affected plant parts, apply organic fungicides, and ensure proper spacing and ventilation.

Prevention: Choose disease-resistant plant varieties, practice crop rotation, and avoid overhead watering.

SOIL PROBLEMS:

Identification: Poor plant growth, yellowing leaves, or stunted development.

Solution: Test soil pH and nutrient levels, amend with compost or organic matter, and follow proper watering practices.

Prevention: Regularly add organic matter, practice no-till gardening, and mulch to improve soil health.

NUTRIENT DEFICIENCIES:

Identification: Yellowing between leaf veins, poor fruit development, or slow growth.

Solution: Apply appropriate organic fertilizers based on plant needs, and ensure proper pH for nutrient availability.

Prevention: Use well-balanced organic fertilizers, rotate crops, and maintain healthy soil.

OVERWATERING OR UNDERWATERING:

Identification: Wilting, yellowing, or dropping leaves.

Solution: Adjust watering frequency and amount based on plant requirements, and improve soil drainage.

Prevention: Use proper irrigation techniques, mulch to retain moisture, and use self-watering containers.

POOR POLLINATION:

Identification: Limited fruit set or misshapen fruits.

Solution: Encourage pollinators by planting pollinator-friendly flowers, avoiding pesticide use, and hand-pollinating if necessary.

Prevention: Provide nesting sites for native bees and other pollinators, and avoid using systemic pesticides.

WEEDS:

Identification: Unwanted plants competing with your garden crops.

Solution: Regularly hand-pull or use mulch to suppress weed growth, and minimize soil disturbance to prevent weed seed germination.

Prevention: Apply thick layers of organic mulch, use weed barriers, and practice good garden hygiene.

ENVIRONMENTAL STRESS:

Identification: Yellowing leaves, leaf burn, or wilting during extreme weather conditions.

Solution: Provide shade, use row covers, or use temporary windbreaks to protect plants from harsh conditions.

Prevention: Choose plant varieties adapted to your climate, provide adequate water, and use proper spacing.

INSUFFICIENT LIGHT:

Identification: Leggy growth, pale leaves, or lack of flowering.

Solution: Choose plants suited for the available light conditions, and consider using supplemental grow lights indoors.

Prevention: Position plants in areas with appropriate sunlight levels, and prune to maintain shape and light penetration.

GARDENER CARE:

Identification: Inconsistent maintenance, neglect, or improper care.

Solution: Regularly inspect and tend to your garden, follow recommended care practices, and keep records of planting and maintenance.

Prevention: Develop a gardening schedule, stay organized, and stay informed about best practices.

Remember, gardening involves trial and error, so don't be discouraged by challenges. Each issue you encounter is an opportunity to learn and improve your gardening skills. Being observant, proactive, and knowledgeable will help you address problems effectively and create a thriving garden.

CHAPTER 10

SEASONS IN GARDEN

Seasons play a significant role in gardening, influencing plant growth, weather conditions, and the tasks you need to perform. Understanding how each season affects your garden allows you to plan and care for your plants effectively. Here's a breakdown of gardening activities and considerations for each season:

SPRING:

Characteristics: Spring is a season of renewal and growth, with warming temperatures and increasing daylight.

Activities:

- Start seeds indoors for warm-season crops.
- Prepare garden beds by amending soil and removing debris.
- Transplant seedlings outdoors as temperatures rise.

- Prune fruit trees and bushes before new growth begins.
- Sow cool-season crops like lettuce, peas, and radishes.
- Address weeds and early pest issues.

SUMMER:

Characteristics: Summer brings the peak of warmth, longer days, and abundant sunshine.

Activities:

- Water regularly, especially during dry spells.
- Mulch to conserve moisture and regulate soil temperature.
- Harvest ripe fruits, vegetables, and herbs.
- Deadhead spent flowers to encourage continuous blooming.
- Monitor for pests and diseases and apply treatments as needed.
- Provide shade for heat-sensitive plants.

- Prune summer-flowering shrubs after they finish blooming.

FALL:

Characteristics: Fall is characterized by cooler temperatures and decreasing daylight, signaling the end of the growing season.

Activities:

- Harvest late-season crops and herbs before frost.
- Plant cool-season crops like broccoli, cabbage, and spinach.
- Collect seeds from non-hybrid plants for next year's planting.
- Clear garden beds, remove spent plants, and add compost.
- Divide perennials and plant spring-blooming bulbs.
- Protect sensitive plants from frost with row covers or cloths.

WINTER:

Characteristics: Winter is a period of dormancy and rest for many plants, with colder temperatures and shorter days.

Activities:

- Plan and organize for the upcoming gardening season.
- Prune dormant fruit trees and shrubs.
- Maintain and clean gardening tools and equipment.
- Provide winter protection for sensitive plants, if necessary.
- Enjoy the tranquility of your garden and reflect on the past season.

Read books, attend workshops, and learn about gardening techniques for the future. Throughout the seasons, it's important to adapt your gardening practices to the changing weather and plant needs. Being attentive to seasonal cues and planning ahead ensures that your garden remains vibrant, productive, and beautiful year-round.

CHAPTER 11

YOUR GARDEN YOUR ZEN

"Your Garden, Your Zen" embodies the idea of creating a peaceful and harmonious space that reflects your personal style, preferences, and inner tranquility. A garden designed with the principles of Zen philosophy can provide a sanctuary for relaxation, contemplation, and a deeper connection to nature. Here's how to cultivate your garden as a place of Zen:

SIMPLIFY AND BALANCE:

- Embrace simplicity in your garden design by using clean lines and minimalistic elements.

- Create balance and harmony through symmetrical arrangements or carefully considered asymmetry.

NATURAL ELEMENTS:

- Incorporate natural elements such as rocks, gravel, sand, and water features to evoke a sense of calm and grounding.
- Arrange rocks in a way that suggests mountains, islands, or other natural formations.

TRANQUIL WATER:

- Install a small pond, fountain, or water basin to provide soothing sounds and a reflective surface.
- Consider adding koi fish or water lilies to enhance the water element.

MINDFUL PLANTING:

- Choose plants that are well-suited to your climate and require minimal maintenance.
- Use a limited color palette, focusing on shades of green and subtle hues to create a serene atmosphere.

MEDITATION SPACES:

- Create designated spots for meditation or quiet contemplation. This could be a bench, a mat, or a designated area for sitting.
- Surround the meditation area with fragrant herbs or flowers to engage the senses.

JAPANESE GARDEN INFLUENCE:

- Draw inspiration from Japanese garden design, which often emphasizes simplicity, asymmetry, and a connection to nature.
- Incorporate elements like bonsai trees, lanterns, and raked gravel patterns (Zen gardens).

AROMATIC PLANTS:

- Plant aromatic herbs like lavender, rosemary, and thyme to infuse the air with calming scents.

- Crush leaves gently to release their natural fragrances.

MINDFUL MAINTENANCE:

- Engage in gardening tasks mindfully, focusing on each action and savoring the experience.
- Regularly tend to your garden to keep it well-maintained and inviting.

PERSONAL TOUCHES:

- Add personal elements like sculptures, wind chimes, or art pieces that hold special meaning to you.
- Create a space that resonates with your own sense of beauty and serenity.

RELAX AND DISCONNECT:

- Dedicate time to unwind, relax, and disconnect from daily stressors in your garden.

- Use your garden as a space for reading, journaling, or simply being present in the moment.

"Your Garden, Your Zen" is about cultivating a space that aligns with your values and brings a sense of tranquility and contentment. By designing and nurturing your garden with intention, you can create a haven that fosters inner peace and a deep connection to the natural world.

CHAPTER 12

CONCLUSION

In the conclusion of your gardening journey, you have the opportunity to reflect on your accomplishments, nurture your passion, and find joy in the process of tending to your garden. Here's how to celebrate your gardening successes, continue learning, and embrace the joys of your beloved garden:

REFLECT AND CELEBRATE:

- Take a moment to appreciate the fruits of your labor. Stand back and admire the beauty and vitality you've brought to your garden.
- Celebrate successful harvests by preparing delicious meals using your homegrown produce.
- Share your gardening achievements with friends and family, and invite them to enjoy the beauty of your garden.

CONTINUING EDUCATION:

- Embrace the role of a lifelong learner. Explore new gardening techniques, plant varieties, and sustainable practices.

- Attend workshops, seminars, and gardening events to expand your knowledge and connect with fellow garden enthusiasts.

- Stay up-to-date with gardening trends and research to enhance your skills and stay inspired.

GROWTH AS A GARDENER:

- View challenges as opportunities for growth. Every setback is a chance to learn and adapt.

- Experiment with new plant combinations, designs, and gardening methods to broaden your expertise.

- Share your experiences and insights with others, whether through online platforms, social media, or local gardening clubs.

MINDFUL CONNECTION:

- Reconnect with the mindfulness and serenity that your garden brings. Spend time tending to your plants with intention and presence.

- Use your garden as a retreat for relaxation, meditation, and self-care.

- Embrace the therapeutic benefits of gardening by immersing yourself in the sights, scents, and sounds of nature.

CULTIVATE GRATITUDE:

- Cultivate a sense of gratitude for the gifts that your garden provides. From fresh produce to a sense of accomplishment, your garden enriches your life in numerous ways.

- Take time to express appreciation for the natural world and the role you play in nurturing it.

CREATE LASTING MEMORIES:

- Capture the beauty of your garden through photography or art, preserving the moments and seasons that bring you joy.

- Share stories and memories related to your garden with loved ones, creating a legacy that spans generations.

CELEBRATING YOUR GARDENING SUCCESSES:

Pause for a moment to appreciate your achievements. From those first sprouting seedlings to the bountiful harvests, each step you've taken has contributed to the beauty and vibrancy of your garden. Whether it's the joy of seeing a flower bloom or the satisfaction of harvesting your own produce, relish in the simple pleasures that gardening offers.

CONTINUING TO LEARN AND GROW:

Gardening is a continuous learning experience. Every season, every plant, and every challenge brings opportunities to expand your knowledge and skills. Stay curious and open to new ideas. Explore different plant varieties, experiment with various techniques, and don't hesitate to seek guidance from fellow gardeners, online communities, and local experts. Remember, even seasoned gardeners are always learning!

EMBRACING THE JOYS OF TENDING YOUR GARDEN:

The heart of gardening lies in the daily rituals of nurturing and care. The gentle touch as you prune a leaf, the satisfaction of watering thirsty plants, and the wonder of watching nature's miracles unfold before your eyes – these are the moments that make gardening a truly magical experience. Embrace the connection you've established with your garden and the sense of calm it brings to your life.

Gardening isn't just about plants; it's about cultivating a sense of responsibility, patience, and mindfulness. It's about understanding the delicate balance of ecosystems and finding harmony within it. As you continue on your gardening journey, remember that you're not just tending to plants – you're nurturing a deeper connection to the earth and the cycles of life.

So, go ahead, step into your garden with renewed enthusiasm. Watch as your efforts blossom into a symphony of colors, scents, and flavors. Cherish the memories you create, the lessons you learn, and the growth you achieve. Your garden is not only a testament to your dedication but also a canvas for your creativity. As you celebrate your gardening successes, continue to learn, and embrace the joys of tending your garden, you'll find that the journey is just as fulfilling as the destination. Your garden is a reflection of your dedication, creativity, and connection to nature—a source of inspiration and renewal that will accompany you throughout the seasons of life.